Contents

UNIVERSITY OF
WOLVERHAMPTON
KNOWLEDGE • INNOVATION • ENTERPRISE

Harrison Learning Centre
City Campus
University of Wolverhampton
St Peter's Square
Wolverhampton WV1 1RH
Telephone: 0845 408 1631
Online Renewals:
www.wlv.ac.uk/lib/myaccount

Deve

rege

Achievi

local a

Alan McGr...   ...d
Victoria Su...

Telephone Renewals: 01902 321333 or 0845 408 1631
Online Renewals: www.wlv.ac.uk/lib/myaccount
Please return this item on or before the last date shown above.
Fines will be charged if items are returned late.
See tariff of fines displayed at the Counter.

The **POLICY**
P P̃
P R E S S

First published in Great Britain in July 2003 by

The Policy Press
Fourth Floor, Beacon House
Queen's Road
Bristol BS8 1QU
UK

Tel no +44 (0)117 331 4054
Fax no +44 (0)117 331 4093
E-mail tpp-info@bristol.ac.uk
www.policypress.org.uk

Published for the Joseph Rowntree Foundation by The Policy Press

ISBN 1 86134 311 6

Alan McGregor is Director of the Training and Employment Research Unit (TERU) at the University of Glasgow, and **Andrea Glass**, **Kevin Higgins**, **Lynne Macdougall** and **Victoria Sutherland** are all Research Fellows within TERU.

The **Joseph Rowntree Foundation** has supported this project as part of its programme of research and innovative development projects, which it hopes will be of value to policy makers, practitioners and service users. The facts presented and views expressed in this report are, however, those of the authors and not necessarily those of the Foundation.

Cover design by Qube Design Associates, Bristol
Printed in Great Britain by Hobbs the Printers Ltd, Southampton

Joined-up working between social inclusion initiatives

Policy background

Social inclusion policy combines two main approaches to dealing with relative disadvantage:

- *area-based* regeneration activities
- programmes targeted at *individuals* in groups at high risk.

Scotland's Social Inclusion Partnerships (SIPs) wrap up both the individual and area-based approaches in a single programme. There is also a third approach that is something of a hybrid where specific groups are targeted and where there is also an area focus. The various issue-specific *zones* dealing with education, employment and health are the best examples of this.

The *area-based* regeneration approach has developed over the last 20 years. The principal current vehicles for regeneration include:

- multisectoral regeneration partnerships, such as those funded under the Single Regeneration Budget (SRB) in England, and SIPs in Scotland;
- the New Deal for Communities in England, focused on the most disadvantaged communities.

New policy frameworks for area regeneration have been developed in the last few years. The Social Exclusion Unit (SEU) was introduced to promote a cross-departmental responsibility for addressing social exclusion, and managed the development of a *National Strategy for Neighbourhood Renewal* (SEU, 2000) and the subsequent *New Commitment* action plan (SEU, 2001). The *National Strategy* is the basis for

many subsequent initiatives and developments (for example, Local Strategic Partnerships [LSPs], neighbourhood management, and so on). In Scotland, the *Social Inclusion Strategy* sets out the framework for the development of inclusion policy and progress is measured against a range of social justice targets and milestones. Communities Scotland has the main responsibility for neighbourhood regeneration at a national level, including the implementation of the Community Regeneration Statement (Scottish Executive, 2002).

Programmes focused on *individuals* in socially excluded groups include the various New Deals:

- for Young People, aged 18 to 24
- for 25 Plus and 50 Plus
- for Disabled People
- for Lone Parents
- for Partners.

These welfare-to-work interventions are the responsibility of the Department for Work and Pensions (DWP), and apply throughout the UK.

The approach in the *zones* targeting employment, education and health issues involves a combined focus on groups with specific disadvantages and resident in particular geographical areas, where the policy thrust on tackling social exclusion calls for:

- innovation
- more effective coordination between agencies
- adding value to existing programmes and service delivery.

The departmental 'ownership' of the zones varies depending on their goals and activities, with the

Employment Zones the responsibility of the DWP.

In the main, these different approaches in the UK have been:

- developed in isolation
- introduced during different time periods, by different governments
- managed by different agencies or organisations.

For all the above reasons, it is likely that there has been a failure to maximise the synergies between the approaches. This raises exciting possibilities in terms of achieving a greater strategic fit between policies for individuals and for areas which would greatly raise the effectiveness and sustainability of *both* the area regeneration and the social inclusion effort.

Joining up in practice

Greater integration between social inclusion initiatives within localities can take a more *strategic* perspective, including:

- exchange of information about programmes and performance to identify gaps or overlaps in provision across the full set of activities;
- agreeing to align strategies and resources to produce benefits for all the inclusion initiatives and their clients;
- isolating barriers to collaboration between the programmes and agencies, which can then be tackled on the ground or communicated to a higher level for action.

LSPs bring together the public, private, voluntary and community sectors to integrate activities in their area. One of the initial tasks of each LSP is to prepare a Local Neighbourhood Renewal Strategy setting out a vision for an area. In Scotland, Community Planning Partnerships (CPPs) are tasked with promoting joined-up working to develop a shared strategic vision in the area. In both instances, enhancing the contribution of *mainstream* service delivery to area regeneration is a central goal.

At a more *operational* level, a closer integration of area-based, welfare-to-work and other social inclusion initiatives and programmes can involve:

- *vertical* joining up of initiatives and programmes to provide assistance to individuals at different stages of their development as they move towards a sustainable, non-excluded position;
- *horizontal* joining up across initiatives and programmes whereby an individual at a single point in time is receiving the services of a range of organisations attacking the different barriers they confront to becoming employed, for example.

Mainstream service delivery also needs to be more effective at the operational level.

Benefits for area regeneration initiatives

The report *Joining it up locally* (DETR, 2000) identifies a number of potential benefits to greater coordination between agencies and organisations at the local, regional and national levels:

- By working with communities, public sector agencies can design appropriate services and harness local capacity to effect change.
- Service providers can develop more flexible services to reflect need.
- Improved coordination can lead to more efficient and effective service delivery.
- There can be improved decision making about resource allocation emphasising preventative expenditure and early intervention.
- Actions that reinforce the work of other agencies can be given priority and constructive actions identified.

There is a consensus among both policy makers and practitioners that the complex problems of social exclusion cannot be identified or addressed using a single agency approach. For ease of administration and delivery the agencies charged with addressing social inclusion tend to be organised on a functional basis, yet this narrow focus can hamper attempts at joined-up working at both strategic and operational levels.

However, we also need to recognise that there can be difficulties in working in a collaborative way. Although neatly integrated projects and programmes are attractive in design and closely collaborating agencies the epitome of common sense, there are costs in the broadest sense and barriers to be overcome before integration and coordination become *self*-sustaining. It is wise to recognise this at the outset, while retaining the vision that we *can* become more effective through a more holistic approach to strategy and delivery.

Key research questions

The research looked at both the benefits and costs of more effective joint working between area regeneration and wider social inclusion initiatives. The key research questions are articulated below.

1 Would a more integrated approach add value to the social inclusion effort?

The assumption is that because these different approaches have been developed in isolation – usually, in fact, in different time periods – the potential for synergy has not been exploited. The outcome is that the resources committed achieve less than they might otherwise. There are then two sub-questions:

- How would greater integration generate more *benefits* for the socially excluded? What are the key linkages or cross-over possibilities between individual and area-based approaches? How do these add value?
- What *good practice examples* of the benefits of greater integration can we uncover? What is the added value that can be demonstrated by these existing more integrated practices?

2 What are the obstacles to greater integration as things stand?

Although there are certainly examples of constructive integration of area-based and individual programmes, there is clearly scope for more to be done. But what stands in the way?

- Many of the 'individual' programmes are top-down and tightly defined. *Do the design features of individual programmes restrict integration?* This is an important issue as it may point to the need for change to be introduced at the national level.

- Rules may allow integration but the *administrative difficulties* (for example, different monitoring systems, mixing government and non-government agencies, and so on) may be an impediment. These obstacles can be harder to discern.
- Are there *too many partnerships?* In a world where there is a plethora of partnerships, the networking (and integrating) possibilities are expanded, but where is the time to do it?
- Are there *technical issues* in the benefits system that limit the potential for integration? For non-benefit specialists, the benefit system is a serious challenge of understanding.

3 How can we achieve more effective integration?

This is a research project designed to guide policy and practice. The outputs are intended to be sharp and well-focused. The key question is, what needs to be done at national and local levels to promote and facilitate more effective integration of social inclusion initiatives?

The report

An extensive set of consultations were carried out in the autumn of 2001 with the staff of a wide range of social inclusion initiatives in nine localities across the UK: Birmingham, Brighton, Glasgow, Leeds, Liverpool, Manchester, Middlesbrough, Nottingham and Southwark. The consultation followed a structured set of key questions addressing the central issue of the integration of area regeneration and wider inclusion interventions.

To make the study manageable, the research focus was mainly on the potential integration of area regeneration programmes with wider welfare-to-work initiatives such as the New Deals and Employment Zones, although we also collected evidence on education, health and childcare interventions. However, many of the findings apply more generally to the scope for more effective joint working between the wide range of more general social inclusion initiatives, mainstream service delivery and area regeneration interventions.

In the remainder of the report:

- Chapter 2 reviews the features of some of the principal social inclusion initiatives and the raft of institutional changes introduced in the last few years;
- Chapter 3 assesses the case study evidence on more integrated approaches and their value;
- Chapter 4 isolates the barriers to more integrated ways of working;
- Chapter 5 discusses what needs to be done to maximise the synergies between area regeneration and wider social inclusion initiatives.

As the infrastructure involved in delivering social inclusion in the UK is in a state of near constant flux, a difficulty for researchers is the change in institutional landscapes between fieldwork and reporting. The best example in this study is the creation in 2002 of a new working age agency – Jobcentre Plus – by combining the Benefits Agency and the Employment Service. In the main, references to the individual agencies in position at the time of the fieldwork have been retained in those chapters of the report which record the findings from the fieldwork process.

Mapping different interventions and institutions

Introduction

In Chapter 1 we noted that a range of new initiatives have been developed since 1997, sharing the inclusion stage with traditional area regeneration initiatives such as the Single Regeneration Budget (SRB). Although there is a great deal of rhetoric about joining up these various interventions to achieve greater effectiveness on behalf of clients, the benefits of this process of more coordinated working are not always articulated. This chapter considers some of the key features of social inclusion initiatives that promote or constrain integration.

Articulation of current inclusion initiatives

Since 1997 there has been a significant expansion in the number of initiatives tackling different manifestations of social exclusion. These built upon and often ran parallel with a well-established set of interventions introduced by previous governments to facilitate neighbourhood regeneration, as well as a range of national programmes for the longer-term unemployed and other socially excluded groups. This section looks at the relationships between these programmes and the factors promoting or inhibiting integration.

A range of factors increases the potential for integrating different initiatives and programmes, including:

- *proximity*
- a common *client group*
- sharing the same *funders* or *organisational affiliations*.

Proximity

There have been shifts in the way that the area-based approaches have been introduced that have affected the geography of implementation (Smith, 1999). As a result of these changes:

- larger areas of a city may be covered by area-based initiatives;
- but there may also be an increasing concentration of initiatives in the most deprived areas.

The upshot is that the most deprived areas may be able to benefit from an array of inclusion programmes and initiatives. In these localities, it is sometimes the case that a whole range of approaches will be overlain.

There is also variation in the geographical scale of the programmes. As Table 1 shows for a selection of the current area-based programmes, some are larger than local authority boundaries while others cover small neighbourhoods. Such variation in scale has a number of consequences for the pattern found at a local level:

- smaller area initiatives may lie wholly within larger zones;
- larger zones may cut across different local authority boundaries;
- zones and other area-based initiatives may or may not be coterminous.

What do these geographical features of scale and proximity suggest about the potential to join up? Clearly, one of the fundamental factors determining the extent of joining up is proximity. The proliferation of area-based approaches, as well as the rolling out of the welfare-to-work approaches such as the New Deals and Employment Zones, indicate that most deprived

Table 1: Major inclusion programmes

Programme	Target area/population	Geography	Client group	Funders	Delivery agent(s)
Single Regeneration Budget (SRB)	The programmes cover areas varying in scale from neighbourhoods to entire towns and cities	England	Diverse, from residents of specific regeneration areas, to unemployed people to adult learners, minority ethnic groups etc	Office of the Deputy Prime Minister	SRB partnerships involve a range of organisations from the voluntary sector, the business community and the local community as well as public sector agencies. SRB is administered at regional level by the Regional Development Agencies
New Deal for Communities	Residents of the most deprived communities in local authority areas	England	All residents in the targeted communities	Office of the Deputy Prime Minister	Local partnerships involving local people, community and voluntary organisations, local authorities, public agencies and businesses
Neighbourhood Renewal Fund	The Fund is available to the 88 most deprived local authorities in England. Within these local authority areas the funding must be spent on the most deprived wards	England	Residents in deprived communities	Office of the Deputy Prime Minister	Local authorities responsible for delivery through LSPs. All authorities must have a local neighbourhood renewal strategy agreed through the LSP. Local authorities, key public sector agencies, voluntary and community organisations, community groups and businesses are represented on LSPs

(contd.../)

Table 1: contd.../

Programme	Target area/population	Geography	Client group	Funders	Delivery agent(s)
Social Inclusion Partnerships (SIPs)	The area-based partnerships aim to assist residents living in the most deprived postcode areas. They vary in scale, ranging from populations of around 4,000 to approximately 40,000	Scotland	Residents of disadvantaged areas	Scottish Executive	Local partnerships including local community, voluntary organisations, businesses, public sector agencies and local authorities
Thematic SIPs	14 thematic SIPs covering communities of interest in diverse geographical areas	Scotland	Diverse, from young people (including those leaving care, who are carers themselves, and who are disaffected or vulnerable to exclusion), minority ethnic groups and prostitutes	Scottish Executive	Each is run by a partnership board usually including representatives of local public sector agencies which have an interest in the target community, local voluntary organisations and local fora such as childcare partnerships and members of the community of interest
Education Action Zones	The zones cover areas of educational under-achievement and/or disadvantage. Generally cover 2-3 secondary schools and their feeder primary schools	England	Pupils and parents facing educational disadvantage	Department for Education and Skills	The schools work in partnership with each other, their local education authority (LEA), local business, parents and community groups
Health Action Zones (HAZs)	Health authorities where there is poor health. Populations included in the zones range from 180,000 to 1.4 million	England	Zones are designed around identifiable local health economies, encompassing primary and secondary care and social services in some of the most deprived parts of England. In total HAZs cover over 13 million people	Department of Health	HAZs are coordinated locally by a partnership board. HAZs are performance-managed by NHS Executive Regional Officers

(contd.../)

Table 1: contd.../

Programme	Target area/population	Geography	Client group	Funders	Delivery agent(s)
Employment Zones	Employment Zones target the long-term unemployed (12 months+ or 18 months+ dependent on zone) claiming Jobseeker's Allowance in high unemployment areas. Each zone typically covers a sizeable area (eg Glasgow and London boroughs such Southwark and Newham)	England, Scotland and Wales	Participation in the zone is mandatory for people who are eligible (either 12 or 18 months unemployed)	Department for Work and Pensions	Mixture of private sector contractors and private–public partnerships
Action Team for Jobs	Action Teams cover specific wards within local authorities that are characterised by low employment rates, high claimant counts and high proportions of minority ethnic groups	England, Scotland and Wales	Any unemployed person living in the Action Team area	Department for Work and Pensions	Action Teams are led by Jobcentre Plus, or in some cases they are led by Employment Zone contractors or by others including private sector recruitment agencies

(contd.../)

Table 1: contd.../

Programme	Target area/population	Geography	Client group	Funders	Delivery agent(s)
New Deals	• *New Deal for Young People:* mandatory for all young people aged 18-24 and unemployed for 6 months or more • *New Deal for 25 Plus:* mandatory for all those aged 25-29 and unemployed for longer than 18 months • *New Deal for Lone Parents:* voluntary programme for all lone parents not working or working less than 16 hours per week • *New Deal for 50 Plus:* voluntary programme open to all people over the age of 50 and claiming one of a range of benefits • *New Deal for Partners of the Unemployed:* voluntary programme offering advice and guidance to partners (if they are aged 18-24) of people receiving Jobseeker's Allowance • *New Deal for Disabled People:* voluntary programme for people with a disability or long-term sickness receiving benefits which do not require them to be available for work	England, Scotland and Wales	Unemployed people in specific eligibility groups	Department for Work and Pensions	Jobcentre Plus primarily responsible for the delivery of the New Deal, but works in partnership with a range of agencies including local authorities, the voluntary sector, trades unions, race equality councils, colleges, careers companies, training providers and employers

areas will be subject to some interventions and possibly a range of them. This creates potential to improve the impact of these programmes by joining up to deliver a more comprehensive and holistic approach. However, the regeneration landscape appears to be becoming *increasingly complex*. If there are too many programmes or initiatives, it may be difficult for practitioners to find the time to create meaningful links with other initiatives, or there may be problems in articulating the various programmes and initiatives.

Variations in the scale of the programmes may also affect the practicalities of joining up. It may be difficult for the *larger programmes to incorporate smaller neighbourhood approaches* at a strategic level. Additionally, practitioners working in smaller initiatives may feel that there is a danger that their initiative will *lose its identity* if it is incorporated into a bigger programme. Such factors clearly have implications for the coordination and delivery of programmes at a local level.

Targeting the same groups

Another area of potential integration exists where programmes target the same socially excluded groups and the same issues. Within these programmes, there are variations in how the socially excluded groups are targeted:

- area regeneration programmes (for example, New Deal for Communities) target all individuals living in a defined area;
- in some zones (for example Health Action Zones) there can be combined focus on groups with specific disadvantages in particular geographical areas.

Programmes and initiatives also overlap in terms of content. There appears to be potential programme overlap in a number of key areas, particularly those improving health and education, and tackling unemployment, as several of the programmes have these common themes. This does not appear to reflect a broadening of content *within* programmes, however. Although the New Deal for Communities tackles four key themes (improving education, improving health, tackling worklessness and crime, thereby improving services and regenerating areas) it is the only

programme to take such a broad approach. The other zones are more focused on specific areas such as education and health.

The development of a range of new programmes, with an overlap in the issues addressed and in the groups they target, appears to offer the potential to develop more sophisticated approaches to tackling the barriers to social inclusion facing particular groups at a neighbourhood level. At a local level, this means that there will be programmes operating that have a specific focus on particular issues as well as programmes offering the possibility of a more comprehensive approach. A shared focus may create common areas of interest, so fostering natural linkages. If this happens, the more comprehensive initiatives may have the opportunity to strengthen their approaches to specific issues (such as health) through the involvement of people working for the zones who may have particular expertise.

Area regeneration programmes focused on particular issues such as childcare, education and health initiatives can help to overcome the specific barriers to the sustainable employment facing particular groups of socially excluded individuals. For example, a local childcare project could link with the New Deal for Lone Parents to offer local childcare solutions for the lone parents participating in the New Deal.

Funders and organisational affiliations

Another area where there may be potential overlap in programmes relates to the organisations that deliver or fund the programmes. A range of key public, private or voluntary and community partners may be involved in several programmes operating at a local level. For example, schools, local education authorities, local businesses and other organisations may be involved in the implementation of Education Action Zones, and the New Deal for Communities will bring together local people, businesses, local authorities, community and voluntary organisations, colleges and schools.

As a consequence, there is potential overlap with certain key partners responsible for or involved in the delivery of several programmes. The large number of delivery agents from different sectors involved in some programmes also indicates the extent to which the necessity for *partnership* as the implementation structure has penetrated the new programmes. It is a requirement of most. Clearly, as their involvement in the range of programmes shows, local authorities have the potential to be a key mechanism for improved coordination and integration. However, this will only happen if there is adequate interdepartmental communication *within* the local authorities involved in the partnerships (as different departments may be involved in different programmes).

Another factor that affects the extent to which this can happen is the *level* at which the various actors are involved. For some of the programmes, such as Employment Zones or Health Action Zones, it may be senior staff who attend the partnership meetings; for others, such as the New Deal or certain SRB programmes, or Sure Start (which is neighbourhood-based), more local workers and indeed local residents may be involved. This clearly has implications for the way that coordination proceeds *within* the programmes and may affect the extent to which partnerships operating different programmes are aware of each other.

Organising for joined-up working

Government and its agencies have introduced a number of institutional mechanisms to promote a more joined-up approach to neighbourhood regeneration – both at a strategic and an operational level. There are also coordinating mechanisms for a range of social inclusion interventions at national, regional and local levels.

Regional Development Agencies

Regional Development Agencies have a remit to work with business, the public sector, the community and voluntary organisations to build links between economic development and social inclusion.

Government Offices for the Regions

Government Offices (GOs) for the Regions were introduced to coordinate the delivery of the

policies of various government departments in the regions of England.

Social Exclusion Unit

The Social Exclusion Unit (SEU) was established in 1997 to work on a range of specific social inclusion projects and to advise on cross-government policy on social inclusion in England. As part of the SEU's *National Strategy for Neighbourhood Renewal* (2000), a number of new government units were established, including:

- the Neighbourhood Renewal Unit set up to implement the *New Commitment to Neighbourhood Renewal* by joining up government at a national level;
- Neighbourhood Renewal Teams based in the GOs to help develop LSPs and join up government policy for local areas.

In 2002, the SEU was relocated from the Cabinet Office to the Office of the Deputy Prime Minister (ODPM). This has brought the SEU into the same government department as other connected policy areas and units including the Neighbourhood Renewal Unit and the Homelessness Directorate.

Regional Co-ordination Unit

The Regional Co-ordination Unit (RCU) was established in 2000 as the *corporate centre* of the GO network. The RCU's activities include:

- ensuring better coordination of area-based initiatives;
- identifying and disseminating best practice across the GO network; and
- providing a regional input into policy development.

Its focus is on the *regional* level – not local or neighbourhood issues.

Local Strategic Partnerships

LSPs have been established in England to integrate and coordinate activity in their area, and include representatives from a range of organisations and agencies involved in regeneration. LSPs are seen as a mechanism to manage the balance of effort between mainstream service delivery and reducing the complexity of local structures and initiatives.

Community Planning Partnerships

Community Planning Partnerships (CPPs) have been set up in Scotland to integrate service delivery at the local authority level and below. As a process, community planning should make the delivery of services more transparent to individuals and neighbourhoods (Lloyd et al, 2001), and help link planning at a national, local and neighbourhood level. In 2004, Scotland's SIPs will become the responsibility of the CPPs.

Communities Scotland

Communities Scotland is tasked with community regeneration through:

*   neighbourhood renewal
*   community empowerment, and
*   housing investment.

To help achieve this, the Area Regeneration Division of the Scottish Executive has moved to Communities Scotland.

Public Service Agreements

Local Public Service Agreements (PSAs) are voluntary agreements between a local authority and the government that aim to improve delivery of local services (DTLR et al, 2001). The local authority makes a commitment to deliver specific improvements in approximately 12 areas of activity and the government makes a commitment to provide specific help (for example, greater flexibility in delivery) and rewards (up to 2.5% of net budget requirement) for these improvements in performance. PSAs are intended to complement other local policies and programmes, for example, Best Value Performance Plans, LSPs, and so on.

New Deal Strategic Partnerships

New Deal Strategic Partnerships (NDSPs) were formed to help the planning and delivery of the

programmes locally. Their main role is as an advisory, monitoring and evaluative body. They have built upon existing local partnership structures, as partners often have a history of joint working, and use existing knowledge and connections to link New Deal with other local initiatives and funding programmes such as the European Social Fund (ESF).

Local Learning Partnerships

Local Learning Partnerships (LLPs) are voluntary, non-statutory groups of training providers and others including local authorities, careers service, trades unions and employers, established in 1999 to improve the coherence and collaboration of post-16 education and training (DfES, 2002). Each LLP addresses the local learning issues they identify as being local priorities, but the core roles are to:

*   support lifelong learning by promoting collaboration between providers; and
*   maximise the contribution of learning to local regeneration.

Overview

Most of the new institutional mechanisms described briefly above have joint working with other key players as some part of their remit. However, one difficulty is that although we now have a plethora of new institutional mechanisms to promote joint working, because these are new structures it is too early to assess their effectiveness. The research by the Department for Transport, Local Government and the Regions (DTLR, 2002) suggests that the new structures contribute to but are not a solution – and in particular the report has major concerns about the failure to bridge effectively between economic development and social inclusion agendas.

Indeed, there is a danger that the proliferation of new institutional forms can itself become a barrier to more effective *operational* integration at the local level, not least because of the resource and time sapping requirements of more formal partnership working within LSPs and CCPs.

A number of the problems involved in generating effective local partnerships are discussed in later chapters of the report, but the next chapter focuses on identifying the benefits that can flow where organisations manage to forge effective working relationships.

3

Benefits flowing from integrated working

Introduction

There are a number of examples of effective joint working between area regeneration and wider social inclusion initiatives across the case study areas. The examples of joint working are discussed in very practical terms to demonstrate *how* effective collaboration can be carried out, as well as drawing out the benefits to all parties than can flow from this. At the end of the chapter we pull together some of the factors which facilitated and supported joint working in the nine localities where the research was focused.

In this chapter, a range of different types of collaborative working arrangements are identified and the benefits of these discussed. A distinction is drawn between:

- *strategic coordination*, where area regeneration initiatives get together with other social inclusion initiatives to discuss gaps and overlaps in services, barriers to more effective collaboration and other issues of mutual interest;
- *joint funding* of projects, programmes or services for socially excluded people to raise the quality of the service that any one individual or household can access;
- *operational integration* of service delivery using a variety of mechanisms with a view to improving access to a wider variety of supports.

However, these are not alternative forms of joint working! The most effective integration of services and initiatives tends to occur where collaboration is taking place at all these levels – strategy, funding and operations.

There are potentially important lessons in this discussion for the organisations – such as Local Strategic Partnerships (LSPs) in England, and Social Inclusion Partnerships (SIPs) and Community Planning Partnerships (CPPs) in Scotland – charged with 'mainstreaming' social inclusion. These organisations need to be able to:

- understand the specific benefits of joint working so that they are able to focus their resources on types of integrated service delivery that will yield the most benefit;
- articulate and 'sell on' the benefits of joint working to a range of different players, and to their staff operating at different levels.

To date, there is an over-emphasis on the general benefits of more coordinated and integrated efforts, but operational staff in particular tend to be more aware of the specific costs for them, for example, in terms of more meetings, with less clarity in their minds around the benefits which accrue. The new Single Local Management Centres (SLMCs) will need to develop a detailed understanding of the benefits and costs of more integrated working arrangements.

Strategic coordination

The highest level of joint working between different types of social inclusion initiatives involves strategic discussions and/or agreements. These strategic collaborations can produce a wide range of benefits. Where there is a strategic overview:

- it becomes easier to 'add value' to existing activity, rather than duplicating or replacing it.

From this can flow:

- resourcing targeted more at unmet need;
- better value for money;
- it helps ensure that individual initiatives are not working against each other;
- it can work to reduce the fragmentation of service delivery, making it easier for the clients to benefit from a comprehensive array of services, offered in a manner that suits the customers and not the suppliers of the services;
- it can facilitate the development of protocols governing relationships between agencies to create the greatest value for common client groups.

We were able to find some examples across the case study localities.

Box 1: Leeds Initiative

The Leeds Initiative provides a strategic approach to the city's long-term regeneration and development. It aims to bring together the diverse partnership groups and provides opportunities for networking and debate. The Initiative encompasses the main public and private economic development agencies, education establishments, voluntary sector and business sectors.

The Employment Service has operational responsibilities for the New Deals and is a member of the Leeds Initiative Regeneration Board, a sub-group of the Leeds Initiative responsible for the appraisal and approval of SRB bids. This appraisal process ensures that all SRB projects:

- are targeted at a demonstrated need;
- 'add value' to existing activity, rather than duplicating or replacing it;
- are realistic in what they are trying to achieve, and deliverable;
- represent good value for money.

One of the main mechanisms for creating and maintaining more effective collaboration at the strategic level is through *overlapping board membership*. A small number of examples of this came up during the fieldwork. In Nottingham, for example:

- the Employment Service is involved at board level in the New Deal for Communities area;
- SRB staff sit on the Sure Start initiative board.

More generally, New Deal Strategic Partnerships (NDSPs) can engage a wide range of partners with inclusion remits.

Provided the board members are sufficiently senior, a number of advantages can flow from overlapping board membership:

- Opportunity is provided for individuals from different types of initiative to be informed about what is happening on the ground.
- The value of different initiatives and programmes can be promoted around the table by individuals with authority and credibility.
- Decisions – formal or informal – to link area-based and group-orientated interventions can be struck, with board members charged to bring the staff and services of their organisations along with the decisions.
- Key individuals will hear what other partners think about the staff and services of their own organisations from peers in other social inclusion initiatives.

The process of joint working can also involve *aligning the different social inclusion strategies* that impact upon regeneration areas, to help point the various organisations in the same direction and promote a more coordinated approach to the deployment of resources. A good example of this is the work done by the Beacons Partnership in Manchester.

Box 2: Beacons for a Brighter Future: East Manchester

The Beacons Partnership operates across a number of neighbourhoods in East Manchester and joins up two major initiatives by managing SRB and New Deal for Communities as a single programme. The SRB bid is a key part of a comprehensive strategy that is required to improve the area as it links together a range of other initiatives and bids, especially New Deal for Communities but also welfare-to-work, the Health Improvement Programme, Best Value and other local strategies:

- City Pride – Manchester, Salford, Trafford and Tameside;

- Manchester City Council's Housing Strategy;
- Education Action Zone – a bid was submitted to improve educational attainment in schools serving Beswick, Openshaw and Clayton;
- Sure Start support for families with children under 4 in Clayton;
- Health Action Zone – although it covers a much wider area than Beacon's European Union Funds;
- Eastlink Investment Corridor – SRB 4. This existing SRB initiative covers Beswick and Openshaw, and also parts of Tameside.

Benefits

- Local access to employment and training advice and guidance.
- Local advice on benefits during transitions to work, removing a potential barrier to taking jobs.

Joint funding or resourcing

Given the deeply embedded nature of the problems flowing from social exclusion, high levels of resourcing are often needed to progress individuals, households and neighbourhoods. If different inclusion programmes and initiatives can pool their resources, this more intensive resourcing can be realised. The benefits of joint funding are many, and include:

- improvements in the scale, quality, range and longevity of services on offer;
- a shared and therefore lower risk for funders which:
  - can lead to more innovative approaches;
  - enables projects to go ahead that a single funding source could not support;
- reduced dependency on a single source of funding for key projects and services;
- a stimulus for the development and delivery of a more holistic approach to tackling exclusion;
- a more effective process for addressing gaps in provision, which should lead to the development of complementary services;
- flexible funding criteria attached to Action Teams for Jobs, which can benefit other more rigidly defined programmes.

A number of practical examples of the value of combining the resources of area regeneration and wider social inclusion initiatives are described below.

Box 3: Glasgow's local economic development companies and Social Inclusion Partnerships

Glasgow has eight local economic development companies (LEDCs) which work closely with the area-based Social Inclusion Partnerships (SIPs) to develop and deliver economic development programmes in the SIP areas. These LEDCs have developed a range of innovative programmes that aim to address the barriers to employment among the most disadvantaged residents, generally using a variety of funding available for specific disadvantaged groups, such as the European Social Fund, and sometimes the New Deal, as well as SIP funds. In effect the LEDCs are a vehicle for joining up the funding available from area-based and individually targeted social inclusion initiatives – and applying this funding in an area regeneration context. There is usually a close working relationship between the staff in both the LEDC and the SIP, and in this way they can influence each other's strategy development and policy work. There are clear benefits from working closely together:

- The LEDCs are also able to access funding to create programmes that can tackle the particular issues that have been identified as barriers to employment (for example, drug use, or lack of childcare and so on). The SIP funding as 'clean' money is a ready source of match funding for European funding.
- SIPs gain from the partnership because LEDCs help them to address some of the harder economic targets they have to address. It is useful to have people with economic development experience on the SIP boards.

Box 4: Action Team for Jobs: Southwark

Action Teams for Jobs (ATfJ) were set up by the Employment Service as an additional resource to address barriers to employment. They are allowed local flexibility to respond to local problems and target appropriate groups within areas. The ATfJ in Southwark is run by Working Links. Its main target is unemployed 16- to 17-year-olds, particularly from minority ethnic groups, those with problems of homelessness and those in receipt of Severe Hardship Benefit.

The ATfJ tries to engage with local programmes to enhance local provision. There are strong links with Southwark Council that gives the ATfJ a link into the SRB-funded projects. The main ways that the ATfJ works with the SRB is through:

- referring clients to SRB projects for pre-employment training, for example, confidence building, English for Speakers of Other Languages (ESOL) and so on;
- provision of luncheon vouchers for parents as an incentive to encourage them to put their children forward and compensate for the benefits that they may lose as a result of their child gaining employment.

As the training is provided through SRB funding, the ATfJ's resources can be used to provide additional support to job seekers, including aftercare. The overall support package is therefore more comprehensive.

Box 5: Granby Toxteth SRB and Dingle Education Action Zone

A number of employment and training courses had been funded by the SRB but had not been completely successful in getting people into jobs. There was a need to focus on employment areas where there were skill shortages. The SRB partnership was simultaneously approached by the Education Action Zone (EAZ) and a local after-school care project to assist with training for classroom assistants. Joint training led to the provision of 16 classroom assistants trained by the after-school project, and at the same time 18 classroom assistant posts were created by the EAZ.

Joining up with New Deal

A number of examples were found where New Deal funding specifically has been invested side by side with area regeneration funds to add value to the services for a common client group.

Benefits for area regeneration initiatives include:

- the deployment of New Deal Environmental Task Force monies to contribute to the process of physical renewal;
- improved quality of training and work experience for local unemployed residents;
- enhanced training inputs, which in turn lead to increased employability and progress for local people, and more sustainable employment opportunities.

Benefits for New Deal, in addition to some of the above, include:

- greater flexibility around individuals' needs than would normally be possible under New Deal;
- potential increases in the length of time that clients can be supported with better potential outcomes as a result;
- help with aftercare services to raise the probability of a sustainable move into work.

Box 6: Cross River Partnership: sustainability and progression in employment

The Cross River Partnership, an established public, private and voluntary sector partnership in London, facilitated a meeting between the key players in the growth sectors of health, hospitality and arts in Southwark, Lambeth and Westminster, to identify areas where SRB resources could add value to the way in which New Deal was being delivered locally. As a result, the Workplace Coordinator Programme was developed. This is funded through SRB and aims to add value to the New Deal programme by employing coordinators to:

- assist unemployed people and New Deal trainees to access, sustain and progress their careers in a number of different occupational areas through careers surgeries;

- support new employees for their first 13 weeks of employment to identify their training needs and provide information about in- and out-of-work support;
- offer coaching for supervisory staff working with New Deal trainees;
- build good relationships with the local Employment Service, community groups, training organisations and employers to enable them both to identify unemployed people wanting to work within the industry and source available vacancies.

The coordinators have access to a training budget to fund individuals on courses to increase their chances of securing sustainable employment.

The workplace coordinators are well placed to address some of the issues that the Employment Service, mainly through lack of time and resources, finds difficult:

- getting employers on board, as employers perceive these coordinators as job brokers who are more professional than their Employment Service counterparts;
- case-loading and marketing individuals, that is, targeting specific individuals for specific jobs on a case-by-case basis;
- accessing a training budget to fund individuals on courses to increase their chances of securing sustainable employment;
- providing longer-term support to individuals to aid job retention;
- widening participation.

The pilot phase of the project funded seven coordinators across the three identified growth sectors and aimed to provide high quality support to a relatively small number of clients. The project was awarded £1.2 million SRB money over three years.

Box 7: Construction training and neighbourhood renewal

In Nottingham, the Employment Service and the City Council are working in partnership with NECTA – a social business in the construction sector – to use the New Deal to provide a construction industry training programme. Although it is a city-wide programme, it focuses on the SRB areas, recruiting from these areas and tendering for any building work in them.

Around 50-80% of the trainees are recruited through the New Deal. Each recruit is offered a 12-month supported employment programme incorporating a 6-month personal development and training period, then 6 months with an employer (either NECTA or another construction employer). During this second 6 months, under the New Deal jobs option, they are able to carry on with their Construction Industry Training Board (CITB) training. After this time trainees continue to receive informal support through the project – helping them to sustain employment and training.

There are a number of benefits that have been realised through this joint working. First, the SRB funding can cover some of the programme costs – ensuring that NECTA can tender for contracts where they are competing against commercial firms. Second, with the assistance of NECTA, the New Deal trainees are supported beyond the time that they would normally be on the New Deal. This makes it more likely that they will be able to sustain employment in the longer term. Another aspect improving the likelihood that trainees will enter better quality jobs is that the project can also assist with the costs of carrying on apprenticeship training, which particularly helps the beneficiaries to access jobs in construction. Additional assistance to buy tools, protective clothing or to cover travel costs is also available through the Action Team for Jobs.

Overall, using the New Deal in conjunction with SRB funding makes the programme more flexible than the mainstream New Deal and therefore more likely to meet specific needs of individuals. Many of the young people accessing the training would have had no access to any other sources of funding which could be used to equip them with the necessary equipment to undertake the training. Around 70% of those who have participated in the scheme have secured jobs. However, it is not only individuals who benefit from this arrangement. The City Council's policy is to maximise the use of local labour in any construction projects taking place in disadvantaged areas, by insisting that contractors use local people. This gives a neighbourhood regeneration focus to government programme funding targeted towards individuals.

Operational integration

Collaborative working arrangements between area regeneration initiatives and other social inclusion initiatives take a number of forms, and examples of these were found around the nine cities which were the focus of the research. Delivering on a joint basis can bring immediate and tangible benefits to the target populations, whether they be defined by geography or group. Operational collaboration can involve one or more of a number of processes:

- sharing information
- sharing premises
- sharing staff and expertise
- sharing clients
- sharing outcomes.

Sharing information

Exchange of information about each other's programmes and initiatives is the essential starting place for a more integrated approach to working between area regeneration and wider social inclusion approaches. This is particularly important as few staff in organisations with a more specialist, single service function – employment, health, education, and so on – are likely to have experience or an understanding of area-based initiatives, and staff of area-based initiatives will be lucky if they had in-depth exposure to any more than one specialist service area.

There are a number of advantages to information sharing:

- Detailed knowledge about the range of services available to excluded client groups prepares the way for future joint working.
- Sharing of information allows area-based initiatives to find out what expertise is available. Frontline area regeneration initiative workers will then be able to provide clients with an improved service, by referring them to provision which they cannot provide themselves.
- The greater availability of information minimises the potential for duplication in service delivery, saves area regeneration and other social inclusion initiative staff investing time developing new projects to deliver

services already available and generally increases the value for money from the resources that are deployed.

Sharing premises

Outreach premises in regeneration areas can service the needs both of neighbourhood initiatives and agencies charged with delivering national social inclusion programmes such as New Deal:

- Delivery through local premises provides a one-stop approach for residents, which gives them easy access to a wide range of services. Clients get services delivered to them on their doorstep and on simple physical access grounds may be more likely to take advantage of them.
- Local delivery enables workers from wider welfare-to-work programmes to reach many more people – and in a less threatening environment.
- Locally based regeneration initiatives can provide local knowledge, contacts, and credibility for a national organisation such as the Employment Service.
- More generally, shared premises increase the number of clients that staff from a range of projects can access. Referral between projects and initiatives is much easier for clients and staff simply because many of the support services are in the same building.
- The co-location of the staff of group-based and area-based initiatives can generate a range of benefits:
  - staff of different organisations can share expertise;
  - it may lessen duplication because staff of one initiative are more aware of what is being offered by others;
  - it can help break down barriers of culture and work practices across organisations.

Box 8: Integrating social inclusion services: East Leeds Family Learning Centre

The East Leeds Family Learning Centre (ELFLC) is based on a learning centre model designed to offer 'local learning provision to meet local needs, linked to employment opportunities'. It is a partnership between Leeds City Council, the Employment Service, further and higher education providers, the Family of Schools Initiative and local employers. The centre provides local people with access to a range of training and employment opportunities:

- A Sure Start programme and an Early Years Centre on site provide childcare for staff and the local community.
- New Deal for Lone Parents advisers and other Employment Service advisers undertake outreach on a surgery basis. Lone Parent advisers are proactive and try to engage clients who would be unlikely to go into the jobcentre. Based on their experience, the Employment Service put a proposal together with Leeds City Council to set up a mobile service for disadvantaged housing estates.
- A Gateway Centre is part of the New Deal initiative providing individuals with a programme of 15-30 hours customised support and training per week.
- A specialist team of careers advisers is working in the centre to assist 16- to 19-year-olds with education, training and employment options.
- A Second Chance School, as part of an innovative European-wide approach, aims to re-engage young people who have left school without any formal qualifications.
- More than 200 courses are delivered on site through a partnership of local colleges.

Benefits:
- The ELFLC built strong links with local employers. This led to the development of the Seacroft Partnership which worked closely with Tesco to secure 500 job opportunities for local people.
- The Gateway Centre at the ELFLC assists residents in an environment in which they are comfortable, and as a result more clients are engaged with learning and employment activities.

Box 9: Castle Vale HAT

Castle Vale Housing Action Trust (CVHAT) was set up to improve housing and general living conditions in Castle Vale in Birmingham, by stimulating employment as well as providing new homes and a shopping centre. CVHAT established a One Stop Centre to offer advice and training to Castle Vale residents. A worker is seconded from the Employment Service who provides a jobs matching service linked closely to local training providers and employers, and CVHAT provides core funding, including funding for training tailored to local employer needs. A number of the people on these courses are funded through New Deal. This mix widens the pool of people available to the employers at the end of the training.

A continual challenge is bending mainstream provision to meet the needs of individuals. CVHAT can provide some funding through its programmes that can help individual circumstances and make the programmes more tailor-made.

Benefits:
- As there is no jobcentre in Castle Vale (the nearest is two bus rides away) the centre can be utilised by local people who may be unused to travelling or are unable to make journeys.
- The Employment Service gets to work at the local level and integrates its work with local providers, helping them to target their job matching service.

Sharing staff and expertise

Drawing on the specialist expertise of the staff of other agencies through secondments can promote the effectiveness of area regeneration initiatives, and also help raise the skills of the staff of more specialist agencies in dealing with clients in poorer communities. There are a number of specific benefits:

- Neighbourhood regeneration initiatives can draw on the expertise of other partners not able to access the client group directly, giving clients access to a service they would otherwise not be prepared to approach.
- Staff of national agencies learn first hand about the realities of area regeneration and

carry this back to their agencies once the secondment is finished.

- Through secondment, lasting bridges are built between the staff of regeneration agencies, welfare to work and social inclusion initiatives.

- Quickly moving clients to the most appropriate support organisations provides a more effective service for clients and saves the time of area-based initiative staff trying to deliver services for which they have limited expertise.

Box 10: Secondments in practice

- The Health Action Zone in West Middlesbrough seconds staff to New Deal for Communities so that the zone can develop a view of how projects could be better delivered on the ground.
- The Employment Service provides secondees to work in Nottingham's SRB areas. The benefit of this arrangement in Bestwood has been greater continuity of Employment Service staff than would normally have been the case. This is seen as being very important in an area where there is a need to build up a strong relationship with clients.

Box 11: Maximising the value of referral for clients: Southwark Employment Zone

Sometimes existing initiatives take on the role of an intermediary. Southwark Employment Zone:

- refers clients with basic skills deficits to SRB projects to provide adult basic education;
- puts its own resources into more direct employability enhancing measures;
- points clients towards New Deal 50 Plus to give them an incentive to take up employment.

Sharing clients: agreeing appropriate referral arrangements

One of the frequent complaints in terms of delivering effective social inclusion services to clients with deeply embedded problems is that:

- referral arrangements between agencies are organised in a haphazard fashion or are well organised in terms of rules and regulations, but these rules are not followed by the frontline staff of the collaborating agencies;
- the staff follow the referral procedure, but clients 'disappear' as they move from one agency to another.

Often poor operation of referral arrangements is a symptom rather than a cause of difficulties between organisations due to, for example, competition or cultural differences.

Nonetheless, where appropriate referral arrangements can be put in place, there are significant benefits to be had:

- Neighbourhood regeneration initiatives can source specialist employment, training or other services for local residents which cannot be delivered by the initiatives.

Sharing outcomes

In a drive to improve performance and increase value for money, the government has placed reliance on measuring outputs and outcomes and allowing resources to flow to good performers through output-related funding. This approach has also become increasingly important in the social inclusion field, particularly in relation to the delivery of national welfare-to-work initiatives such as some of the New Deals and Employment Zones.

When area-based and other social inclusion initiatives are able to share outcomes, there is mutual benefit to be gained from organisations working more closely, for example, by referring clients to each other.

Box 12: The Employment Service and Glasgow's local economic development companies

The Employment Service has a service-level agreement with the LEDCs in Glasgow – which typically help to deliver the employment and training aspects of the agendas of the city's area-based SIPs. The Employment Service refers clients to the services and projects these local companies deliver, and in return they are obliged to notify the Employment Service when any of these clients leave and are in work 13 weeks after leaving. The Employment Service is then able to claim a job outcome – as is the LEDC in relation to its funders. The same arrangement operates when the Employment Service pays LEDCs to deliver its programmes, but here the obligation to report back on positive job outcomes is contractual.

Mechanisms for promoting integration: working through intermediaries

A number of the best examples of effective joint working between area regeneration and wider social inclusion initiatives were brokered and managed by intermediaries or subsidiary organisations able to package up a range of inclusion resources from funders and programmes.

Box 13: Developing subsidiaries: Jobs, Education and Training (JET) centres

The Speke–Garston Partnership established a JET team to:

- work with local business to assess and supply their demands through helping them to train their existing workforce;
- assist local unemployed people to take up jobs.

In 2001, the JET approach was rolled out across Liverpool.

JETs are based in and well connected to local communities. They aim to serve individuals who do not often leave their local neighbourhood and who would be unlikely to use jobcentres. In particular, they aim to provide services for people, such as lone parents, not in receipt of 'active' benefits. As it is not a statutory body the local residents feel more comfortable about visiting the centre, and less fearful of benefits sanctions being imposed as a result of their visit.

The JET can deliver bespoke training for the local employers based on their needs and the job opportunities that are being created. Their role has been expanded and adapted to meet the requirements of new programmes such as the New Deal and Employment Zone. They provide services across South Liverpool with support from Liverpool Partnership Group's Round 6 SRB programme. There are also JETs in Liverpool North and Bootle/Sefton.

The JET initiative:

- formed the Speke–Garston New Deal Consortium, which was successful in a bid to supply the Gateway provision;
- was awarded a personal adviser contract for the prototype Employment Zone. They have created linkages between this work and the other JET projects;
- entered joint working with the Employment Service, the Employment Zone and the Learning and Skills Council to draw up a protocol to present a united face to the employers who wanted a one-stop service.

Benefits:
Both the JET service and the Employment Service identify benefits flowing from their joint work:

- The JET centres have a comparatively small staffing complement and yet they deal with some very large-scale recruitment projects. It is very useful for them to have the *additional personnel* who can be supplied by the Employment Service when they are dealing with large recruitment projects.
- The JET helps the Employment Service deliver results. Mainly, clients are able to access additional assistance through the JETs that would be unavailable under statutory provision – this gives their service a bit more *flexibility*.

Joining up can improve access to resources and expertise to tackle issues where regeneration partnerships have little experience. Partnerships cannot deliver everything themselves and specialists can push initiatives forward.

Box 14: Creating intermediaries: Employment and Regeneration Partnership Ltd

Manchester Enterprises was formed through a partnership between four local authorities: the Chamber of Commerce and Industry, Manchester TEC Ltd, Manchester Careers Partnership and MIDAS. Employment and Regeneration Partnership Ltd (ERP) is one of the operating companies of Manchester Enterprises. Its initiatives include the following:

- *Employment Centres:* the ERP runs locally focused Employment Centres providing advice and guidance services, training, intermediate labour markets (ILMs), job matching and ongoing support.
- *ILM:* ERP run an ILM which draws money from SRB, European Social Fund and New Deal. The New Deal funding adds an economic inclusion element.
- *Employment Service:* a pilot scheme has been run locating Employment Service and ERP staff together in jobcentres and in ERP premises. Local people can sign on in Employment Centres and access ERP services. This reaches individuals who may not use jobcentres, or leave the local area.
- *Community and Environmental Employment* is a programme to enhance the New Deal for Young People, replacing the Voluntary Sector and Environmental Task Force options. The programme enhances New Deal by offering young people paid employment combined with training and personal support for 12 months. It draws funding from SRB, New Deal and the European Social Fund.

Benefits:
- Residents have local access to Employment Service and ERP services in one place. This can help reach non-Jobseeker's Allowance claimants and people who seldom use jobcentres.
- Integrated working adds value to projects, for example, by using New Deal and European Social Fund funding to enhance the ILM programmes.

Factors promoting more integrated working

This chapter demonstrates clearly the benefits to be gained from more integrated working between area regeneration initiatives and more general social inclusion projects and programmes, such as the various New Deals. The Department for Transport, Local Government and the Regions (DTLR, 2002) identified a range of factors which promote joint working, including:

- traditions in localities of networking and collaborative working;
- the laying down of explicit requirements for collaboration, laid down and backed up at a senior level by the various parties;
- shared ownership among the key players of collaborative efforts and their effective involvement in running the process.

The many examples in this chapter also help illustrate the circumstances and approaches that promote joint working. These include:

- agreeing some *strategic alignment* between the players in a locality responsible for delivering different initiatives;
- supporting this through the development of *overlapping board membership* across the main players;
- looking for opportunities to *put the resources of different programmes and initiatives side by side* to create more effective services for clients and to raise the likelihood of each organisation achieving its targets;
- exploiting all opportunities for *more effective and meaningful operational collaboration*, often stimulated by:
  - sharing premises in order to reach clients more effectively;
  - sourcing expertise which does not exist in the host organisation to offer clients a better service;
  - developing good quality referral arrangements, again to provide services for clients which the organisation cannot deliver easily;
  - showing a willingness to share the outcomes achieved for clients with other organisations because this makes it easier to achieve the organisation's own targets.

It is important to recognise, particularly in relation to operational integration, that there needs to be clear benefits for the staff involved which overcome the greater complexity associated with working jointly with other agencies and organisations.

However, given the potential for benefit, why then do we not see more joint working? The next chapter explores some of the main barriers. Chapter 5 will then explore in greater detail the questions of what needs to be done and by whom to promote joint working between area regeneration and wider inclusion initiatives.

4

Barriers to integration

Introduction

The last chapter showed the many benefits that can flow from inclusion initiatives working more closely together – so why does this not happen more often? A collection of barriers has been identified in a number of recent studies (Audit Commission, 2002; Maclennan, 2000; RCU, 2002a; DTLR, 2002). The fieldwork in the case study localities confirmed the salience of these barriers.

Evidence from the case study localities

To inform our understanding of the barriers to integrating area-based and other measures to promote social inclusion, this chapter focuses on the specific barriers identified in the case study localities which impede more joined-up working between neighbourhood regeneration initiatives, the various zones, flagship welfare-to-work initiatives such as the New Deals, and other social inclusion interventions. Many of the barriers will be familiar to staff struggling at the frontline with the more general issue of why we do not have more joined-up government and service delivery in the social inclusion area and beyond.

Top-down programmes

One of the major problems in achieving a more effective collaboration between neighbourhood regeneration and other inclusion initiatives is the top-down nature of many of the post-1997 welfare-to-work developments such as the New Deals and the various zones. In a sense, most initiatives are top-down as the bulk of the funding comes from central government, and Maclennan (2000) criticises the SEU's *National Strategy* in part on the grounds that it starts from a centralised view of neighbourhood change and its drivers.

The main barriers uncovered in the case study localities surround a range of characteristics of top-down initiatives:

- they tend to be limited in their local flexibilities;
- even where bids for local delivery are invited (for example, with Employment Zones) the design is closely defined by central government;
- there is a problem of connecting national organisations to local solutions. Understanding of the local level is low among national organisations;
- national agencies have difficulty responding quickly and flexibly to local needs, and tend to require central departmental permission for even small-scale local deviations from the model;
- national programmes tend to place a strong focus on measuring more immediate outcomes rather than longer-term impacts;
- in a number of welfare-to-work initiatives participation of unemployed people is sometimes mandatory, conflicting with the ethos of community involvement and empowerment which runs through most area regeneration initiatives;
- the principal delivery agency, in the case of the New Deals, is a national agency – the Employment Service – often viewed with distrust by residents of poorer neighbourhoods and the staff working to regenerate their areas.

All of these features make it difficult to provide an effective fit between locally driven area regeneration approaches and national welfare-to-work and other social inclusion initiatives.

Government departments are not joined up

Although government creates most of our inclusion initiatives from a distance and is strong on the rhetoric of more integrated working, a persistent theme throughout our consultations around the country was the difficulty emanating from the failure of government *at the centre* to adopt a more joined-up approach to promoting social inclusion. This is a problem within area regeneration, as well as between area regeneration and wider social inclusion interventions, as demonstrated convincingly by Carley et al (2000) and DTLR (2002). In terms of wider social inclusion initiatives a number of examples were cited in our research:

- Segmentation between broad policy delivery areas makes it hard to achieve synergies across area regeneration and other social inclusion programmes. There is a lack of understanding of shared problems and the potential for joint solutions.
- Each department tends to have different systems and requires separate information for auditing and monitoring purposes. This makes it difficult for the programmes to join up at the local level – and also imposes significant administrative burdens on organisations trying to work with more than one national programme. Add in the auditing requirements of the various European funds and the question becomes, for an area regeneration initiative, does the increased funding compensate for the added administrative hassle?
- In the Scottish context, some SIPs highlighted the difficulty of getting local authority education departments to engage effectively, and attributed this in part to departmentalism within the institution of regional governance where the Scottish Executive's Education Department is seen to be run as an entity quite separate from other cognate departments, including the one responsible for area regeneration.
- The lack of clear and effective integration between central government departments, their regional agencies and other regional

government machinery conflicts with the rhetoric around joined-up government, and sends negative signals down to the regional and local tiers of their organisations. Local agencies not keen for whatever reason to partner with others can simply point up the line to justify their stance.

Too many players and initiatives

"Middlesbrough has more visions than Mother Theresa – and more pilots than British Airways."

The message from Middlesbrough was echoed throughout all the case study localities. There are too many initiatives and players involved in area regeneration and social inclusion which makes it extremely difficult to find out what is going on at the local level. This, in turn, creates a barrier to effective integration of service delivery:

- An Employment Service manager interviewed had been in post for 18 months but still found it very hard to understand the roles played by all the local agencies and identify which funding streams were available in his area. Some Employment Service districts contain a large number of SRB or SIP projects, as well as the plethora of other neighbourhood-based initiatives, zones, and so on, but it is very difficult and time-consuming to obtain comprehensive information about all of them and it is not routinely provided.
- Even when it is possible to understand the inclusion scene, there are too many neighbourhood projects for the Employment Service, Employment Zones or other agencies with a wider spatial remit to dedicate time and resources in terms of simple engagement, never mind integration of service delivery. Meetings use up valuable time and resources. Organisations need to try and identify where joint working can add value: "we must prioritise – let's not engage in partnership working for the sake of it".
- The Glasgow Alliance, responsible for the city's SIPs, argues that there are too many players working at a neighbourhood level. This means that area regeneration and other social inclusion initiatives are: "working in an increasingly cluttered environment, with all the initiatives looking quite similar".

The findings echo the views of the Performance and Innovation Unit (2000), the Audit Commission (2002) and the RCU (2002a), which see the proliferation of area-based initiatives as a major constraint on operational effectiveness. Widening this out to consider the full range of social inclusion interventions simply reinforces the point.

Different priorities

A widespread barrier to joining up different types of social inclusion initiative is the lack of a common set of priorities. This barrier was raised often and by a wide range of organisations, and it leads to a range of fundamental difficulties. Where organisations and programmes have different priorities it limits the scope for joint action which is in their mutual interests, or in the interests of their clients. This can manifest itself in a number of different ways:

- Different programmes and initiatives have different client groups. For example, New Deal for Young People is focused on 18- to 24-year-olds who meet specific criteria in terms of type of benefit claimed and length of unemployment, whereas neighbourhood regeneration initiatives focus on local residents largely irrespective of personal characteristics. With the decline in unemployment in the UK the number of people meeting the New Deal for Young People eligibility criteria has fallen, and in any specific neighbourhood there may be relatively few of them. This means that:
  ‣ for the regeneration initiative, New Deal is going to be of relevance for only a small proportion of their client group;
  ‣ for the Employment Service, there are relatively few clients in any specific regeneration area.
  In neither instance is there much incentive to invest in joint working.
- Even where initiatives are ostensibly working in the same general direction, different types of priorities can still intervene. For example, Employment Zones and SRB employment projects generally have the objective of getting people into work and reducing long-term unemployment in their respective areas. However, the Employment Zones are much more focused on getting people into work, whereas local employment projects tend to be more concerned about raising employability in

the longer term. For this reason Employment Zones have been sceptical about the value of lengthy, SRB-funded training programmes and intermediate labour market projects as vehicles for targeting job entry barriers.

- The reality is that many wider social inclusion initiatives, and indeed inclusion services which have local authority or wider geographical remits, do not tend to see providing a different kind of service into regeneration areas as part of their remit. It is simply not perceived as their core business.
- As well as the geographical mismatch of priorities there are issues about the linkages between initiatives which provide a specific type of service delivery, for example, around health, crime and safety, and so on. Employment-related initiatives and agencies often struggle to see the relevance of these other services in terms of meeting the priorities that they have been set.
- Shifting priorities complicate the issue. Education Action Zone staff in several of the case study areas described how changes in priorities had made it difficult for them to develop joint working with neighbourhood-focused projects or programmes targeted towards individuals. They reported how the zone agenda had moved away from supporting innovative projects which would help schools to make an impact on the wider environment in which they operate (hence opportunities to develop neighbourhood-focused programmes) towards a narrower focus on raising attainment. This reduced the incentive for zones to work with local partners.

Different time-scales

Many social inclusion initiatives operate to different time-scales and this introduces another range of problems or barriers to joining up more effectively:

- The fully fledged Employment Zones were set up with fixed lives, although these were then extended for the initial 15 zones. However, they are generally operating with a time-scale for delivery of their targets of up to two years, which means that they will focus their resources on clients who can make a contribution to their targets within these time-scales. The New Deals generally operate to targets set on an operating year basis.

- Neighbourhood regeneration initiatives generally work to much longer time-scales which allow them to deploy resources in a different way. Whereas early gains are desirable, the initiatives will be evaluated in terms of the sustainability of the benefits that they have been able to introduce to their localities. This may make them less interested in those clients closer to the labour market who may find work on their own. They may place more emphasis on residents with more deeply embedded problems.

Contrasting the above two cases it is easy to see how there can often be a lack of fit between the efforts of the two types of organisations.

Mismatch between boundaries

The UK's social inclusion initiatives operate within very different sets of geographies, ranging from the New Deals where effectively there is no geographical distinction in terms of priority and delivery, down to highly focused area regeneration initiatives, such as New Deal for Communities. This is an inevitable feature of any strategic approach to inclusion which builds in priorities based on neighbourhood characteristics. However, it does create barriers for joint working:

- SRB and New Deal for Communities funding is postcode specific. This makes it difficult for organisations without a neighbourhood focus to work alongside them. It is difficult for the Employment Service to explain to clients that they are "caught up in a postcode lottery".
- In Liverpool, the Action Teams for Jobs do not correspond with the regeneration geography. Prior to their introduction there were no consultations with the city council about the areas they would cover. This means that they can cut across partnership and joint working in some areas and add another layer for employers, job seekers and local partnerships: "Action Teams for Jobs highlight an unresolved tension between central government encouragement of joint working and a lack of integration of government departments".

Output and target-driven programmes

Increasingly, government policy has favoured performance measurement and management systems which lean heavily on the achievement of specific targets or outcomes within a given budget. The social inclusion field is no different in this regard. The Department for Transport, Local Government and the Regions (DTLR, 2002) noted the difficulties of creating joint working between initiatives which were driven to deliver shorter run outputs versus other interventions, where the focus was on longer-term outcomes.

The issue of targets and outputs was frequently raised as a barrier to joining up different types of inclusion initiatives during the fieldwork. A number of difficulties were identified:

- For the initiatives focusing on individuals who are members of targeted groups, such as the New Deals, an individual living in a regeneration area assisted by New Deal carries exactly the same weight as one not living in a regeneration area, that is, there is no incentive to work harder to promote the employability of the individual in a regeneration area. Indeed, targets tend to focus attention on those individuals, groups and localities where results can be achieved most readily, and these tend not to be regeneration areas. An Employment Service interviewee noted that: "We are target driven and have a business to run. While long-term investment can reap rewards, shorter-term investment with no visible benefit can seldom be justified".
- The emphasis on meeting specific targets is generally allied with a relatively tight time-scale for achieving this. Targets are often set to be met within a calendar or financial year setting. Where clients require a longer-term investment which may not yield a contribution to targets within this time period, as will often be the case with individuals living in poorer communities with more deeply embedded problems, there is little incentive to support that particular client.
- In instances where only one organisation is able to claim an outcome against a specific client, this offers little incentive for agencies to cooperate other than through direct financial contribution paid for any service they have offered.

Box 15: Meeting Employment Service targets

In the majority of the case study areas there was a clear perception that a strong focus on the achievement of targets can inhibit the Employment Service becoming involved:

- in development work for which there are no tangible outcomes;
- in work that make their targets more difficult to achieve;
- with organisations which might claim some of their successes.

Examples of each of these barriers are given overleaf:

No tangible outcomes
Being target-driven mitigates particularly against joint working with neighbourhood organisations because it was perceived that this type of work is time and resource consuming. Interviews with Employment Service staff in one locality revealed that staff faced a dilemma. On the one hand, they were willing to work closely with neighbourhood organisations at local level, but they also recognised that it takes time to build up trust and good relationships between organisations. There are no tangible outcomes from this work.

Making achieving targets more difficult
The Employment Service's priority is to get unemployed clients into jobs, largely through mandatory programmes. Although the Employment Service in one of the case study localities had supported the local employment initiatives in a number of SRB-funded partnership areas through seconding staff, they have been under increasing pressure to reduce their commitment to the SRB programmes in three of the areas. In the partnership areas, the Employment Service simply could not match the targets reached in their mainstream offices.

Claiming outcomes in the locality
In one locality, there is an Action Team for Jobs operating within the New Deal for Communities area. The Action Team is managed by the Employment Zone. The Employment Service has come to an arrangement with the local training and employment initiatives to act as intermediaries and deliver services on their behalf.

In these circumstances the Employment Service and the local initiatives claim client outcomes jointly. However, there is no arrangement in place to do this with the Action Teams for Jobs which is managed by the Zone, which is a major disincentive to joint working.

The new combined working age agency – Jobcentre Plus – has introduced a points system which begins to address this issue by allocating points to different types of clients placed in jobs, with the highest points allocated to priority groups such as lone parents and disabled people. Although additional points are awarded for clients placed in work in Employment Zones and the 30 local authority districts with the worst labour market conditions, there is no points premium for successful job entries for clients resident in, for example, SRB or SIP areas – but this could easily be introduced to cement firmer joint working arrangements between employability programmes and neighbourhood regeneration.

Lack of local flexibilities

The interviews raised concerns relating to the way that strict eligibility rules attached to some programmes can restrict take-up of the training opportunities that might be on offer through neighbourhood projects. Eligibility rules could restrict access to both Employment Service programmes and neighbourhood-based programmes, and make both sets of organisations reluctant to develop a joint approach:

- In order to qualify for Jobseeker's Allowance unemployed clients may only undertake a maximum of 16 hours training or education before they lose their right to claim. In many case study areas interviewees reported that this makes it impossible for clients living in disadvantaged neighbourhoods to make use of some of their local projects because they would be unable to take up the training opportunities which may be on offer and still claim their benefits.
- Funding restrictions applicable to government agencies mean that the Employment Service cannot use SRB or New Deal for Communities funding to pay for additional staff, even if they are not undertaking usual Employment Service duties. If the Employment Service does want

to develop specific projects to tackle local needs, it must bid for additional money from the Treasury. In one area, the Employment Service has overcome this barrier by seconding individuals to partner organisations and then invoicing them for the staff time, but this is time-consuming and bureaucratic.

Barriers between agencies and neighbourhood initiatives

It was clear from our fieldwork that there are significant cultural and related barriers between some of the more mainstream government agencies and area regeneration initiatives.

Organisational culture clash

Joining up between initiatives and programmes involves joining up between *organisations*. It is in the nature of organisations, particularly well-established ones, that they develop different cultures, operating environments, management styles and ways of working with their clients. Indeed, the drive to set up locally based, community focused neighbourhood regeneration initiatives over the years was in part a response to the failure of national and local government agencies to interact effectively with the poorest communities. These local initiatives have built up expertise and credibility in their local communities, and ways of working which help them attract, retain and progress clients.

Maclennan (2000) highlighted the tendency of government to underestimate the problems that confront attempts to coordinate working across organisations with very different cultures and organisational ethos, and the Audit Commission (2002) viewed entrenched organisational cultures as a serious barrier to the effective implementation of the Neighbourhood Renewal Strategy. Rodger et al (2000) drew similar conclusions in a study of New Deal Strategic Partnerships which highlighted the very different cultures of the Employment Service and local regeneration initiatives.

The research in the case study localities confirmed a number of the findings of those studies:

- Organisations such as the Employment Service and Benefits Agency are often viewed with suspicion by the residents of low-income neighbourhoods, and by the staff of local initiatives working on their behalf who perceive the role of these agencies as one of policing the benefits system rather than necessarily providing services which will raise employability. This lack of trust in the community can also extend to other agencies such as the police, health service and local authority housing and other departments.
- The Employment Service focus on mainly mandatory programmes for the unemployed rests uneasily with neighbourhood employment initiatives where services are often voluntary and client-focused. One member of staff working in a New Deal for Communities project claimed that residents do not want Employment Service representation on neighbourhood projects for this reason.
- As a consequence of the above features, neighbourhood regeneration initiatives, seeking to interact more effectively with national agencies and programmes, run the risk of alienating their client group and eroding the bridges that they have built with their communities over the long term. Effectively this means that there is a need for significant benefit for neighbourhood regeneration agencies flowing from a closer association with, for example, New Deal if greater joined-up working is to be achieved and sustained.

Staff attitudes, knowledge and skills

There are other kinds of barriers more to do with the attitudes, knowledge and skills of staff. Research by the Tavistock Institute (1999), for example, suggested that Employment Service staff found it difficult to engage effectively in partnership working. A number of related issues were raised in the case study localities:

- There is a perception within area regeneration initiatives that the Employment Service fails to engage fully with the community and appears to have little knowledge or understanding of what community-based organisations are doing. As we noted earlier, however, it is difficult for the Employment Service and other agencies with comprehensive geographical coverage to have good quality and up-to-date knowledge when there is a plethora of area-based regeneration initiatives on their patch.

- Agencies have very different working conditions: "It is hard to get the Benefits Agency involved at neighbourhood level as they are used to having screens between them and their clients". Involving statutory agencies may require a shift in working practices, although the new Jobcentre Plus may help tackle a number of these issues as the enhanced, more client-friendly offices are rolled out across the UK.

- The staff of area regeneration initiatives tend as a matter of course to develop partnership working skills as they have to work closely with local community organisations and their funders (local authorities, and so on). For national agencies, the work process is more contained and hierarchically organised. In this context, partnership skills do not develop as naturally.

- Building local contacts and working relationships is difficult enough between neighbourhood projects and the Employment Service, but high staff turnover rates exacerbate this. Employment Service staff are perceived to be frequently reallocated, making it difficult for them to develop good local knowledge and contacts, at the same time reducing the ability of the staff of neighbourhood regeneration initiatives to build constructive budgets with their local job centre.

The Audit Commission (2002) highlighted the problems of skill deficits among key staff, and the above examples underline this, but also illustrate the complexity of some of the skill sets required.

Suspicion of private sector operators

A number of the major welfare-to-work programmes have used private sector contractors to deliver services. The public sector is often suspicious of private sector involvement in regeneration and inclusion initiatives; partners fear both their motives and successes: "Initiatives are threatened by achievement and use this as an excuse to keep the private sector out". In addition, neighbourhood-based projects are dependent upon the close working relationships which they build up with the local community. There is a perception that SRB-type projects are

not comfortable with the involvement of private companies because their clients may be suspicious of employment agencies which they perceive to offer short-term, low-paid job opportunities.

Specific difficulties with Employment Zones and New Deal

Across the case study areas, interviewees working in neighbourhood regeneration programmes were often reluctant to use the New Deal or Employment Zones in the development of programmes for a range of reasons, including poor previous experiences and a feeling that these programmes do not meet the needs of their particular client groups.

Box 16: Value of New Deal and Employment Zones for regeneration areas

Glasgow's local economic development companies (LEDCs) identified a range of issues that have inhibited the extent to which national programmes such as the New Deal or the Employment Zones are suitable to provide funding for their area-based employment programmes.

- Employment Zones and New Deal cannot provide for the needs of many of the clients who live in regeneration areas. They need a greater amount of support, and this costs more money than these programmes can devote.
- It is difficult to provide the flexibility of service that suits the circumstances of particular clients in regeneration areas within the context of national programmes.
- Some of the programmes that they believe promote client personal development and eventual employability (for example, stress relief) would not be allowable under the New Deal.
- The mandatory nature of the programmes is off-putting to potential clients.
- New Deal and Employment Zone personal advisers continue to exert too much control over where a client goes. If they do not think that a particular type of provision will help to meet their targets then they may not refer a client.

- The New Deal has inadequate links with employers.
- The New Deal has significant *bureaucracy*, which is time-consuming especially for small local projects who want to develop short-term focused local projects.

Liverpool City Council, supported by SRB funding, operate an intermediate labour market (ILM) programme providing training and employment opportunities in sports and recreation to unemployed people at the Elaine Norrie Sports Centre in the Eldonian Village in Liverpool. This is a programme that would offer ideal opportunities to zone clients, yet there is no incentive for the zone to use this as training provision. Although transferring clients to an ILM programme would reduce costs for the zone in the short term, it is not an optimum use of zone funds because they would not be able to claim a successful outcome payment. As a gesture, recognising the specific needs of a handful of clients, around 25 individuals out of the 6,500 on the zone have been referred to this programme. This could not be justified economically with larger numbers.

The DWP (2001) Green Paper, *Towards full employment in a modern society*, introduced a number of changes to New Deal, implemented in 2002, with three key new points of focus:

- more employer involvement
- more flexibility for advisers
- more support for those needing extra help.

These developments may make the fit with neighbourhood regeneration initiatives easier to achieve. The greater flexibility for advisers and the more individually tailored assistance now on offer to clients could help to address many of the perceived barriers to collaboration reported by consultees.

Competition for clients and protection of interest

In a situation where a number of national inclusion programmes are superimposed upon an existing diversity of area-based regeneration initiatives, there can be issues about competition in the 'marketplace':

- The most obvious competition is for *clients*, clearly. If programmes or initiatives are unable to process a significant number of clients their ability to meet their targets is compromised.
- For initiatives seeking to link unemployed people to jobs there is also competition for the *vacancies* that the employers have to offer.
- In the last analysis much of this comes down to competition for *funding* from local authorities, national government and from Europe.

The introduction of New Deal and Employment Zones produced serious knock-on effects for some area-based employment and training initiatives.

Although the protective reaction is not what the government is seeking, a competitive response may well be to the benefit of residents of regeneration areas as some organisations seek to improve their performance with a view to securing their long-term future. However, what these organisations are generally not prepared to do is make life easy for the new agencies and programmes:

- The early reaction of the Employment Service to the establishment of the fully fledged Employment Zones was competitive rather than collaborative, notwithstanding the fact that both organisations were working in broad terms to raise the employment prospects of the longer-term unemployed.
- The relationship between the Employment Zones and the area regeneration partnerships of one kind or another has been tense because the zones are the new players in town with a geographical scope that overlaps with, although it is typically wider than, the areas covered by SRBs, SIPs and other area regeneration initiatives.
- The Employment Service and neighbourhood-based projects dealing with employment and recruitment tend to perceive each other as competition. A neighbourhood employment project, such as At Work in Middlesbrough, has been successful in terms of securing vacancies for unemployed clients. There is a tension here with the Employment Service job centres which can be constructive, pushing up standards all round, or simply lead to defensive behaviour and low levels of integrated service delivery.

- When different initiatives end up competing fiercely for clients, the numbers are spread too thin and the viability of providers and projects is threatened, as Box 17 illustrates.

Box 17: Maintaining viable provision

Concern was expressed in Nottingham that the Employment Zone could potentially squeeze long-term unemployed clients aged 25 or over to a level at which it would be difficult for the Employment Service to provide meaningful provision for clients under New Deal 25 Plus. The per head cost of contracting provision for the Employment Service rises as the client group decreases in size. This makes it difficult to keep small training providers on board and restricts the Employment Service to using the larger providers that can build more flexibility into what they offer. As long as the zone is in existence it is difficult to see how this could be overcome given that the zone automatically takes the clients away from the Employment Service. In due course, the government 'solved' this problem by passing the management of New Deal 25 Plus to Employment Zones in the areas where they operate.

Joint working is time and resource consuming

Even if individual organisations and initiatives are prepared to make the effort, time and resources become a constraint on joined-up working. The problems here include:

- gaining a fuller understanding of what other initiatives can contribute to your client group;
- developing some sense of the normal working arrangements of other initiatives and their staff;
- assessing how to engage more effectively with these initiatives on behalf of your clients; and
- coping with the time spent in meeting with other initiatives and their staff.

All of these can be extremely demanding of organisations who already work to a tight resource budget and demanding time-scales.

Lack of interest or incentive

In the last analysis, irrespective of whether all the other appropriate conditions are in place, there needs to be an incentive for area regeneration and other welfare-to-work initiatives to join up on a more effective basis. Admittedly such an incentive could operate at a number of levels but, given the fact that collaborative working carries a cost in terms of the time and resource required to identify the scope for collaboration, make the connections, and sustain these over time, benefit needs to flow to all collaborating parties. In the consultations around the UK, there was no strong sense that neighbourhood regeneration initiatives and wider social inclusion approaches valued working more closely together – and organisations were able to bring forward plenty of good reasons for not collaborating.

A summary of the barriers to integration

The box overleaf summarises some of the key barriers to the more effective integration of area regeneration and welfare-to-work initiatives, based on the views of two sets of players, area regeneration and welfare-to-work initiatives.

Box 18: Key barriers to integration

		Area regeneration	Welfare-to-work programmes
1	No one told us to work together	✔	✔
2	Not sure our superiors want us to work together		✔
3	Detracts from meeting our targets	✔	✔
4	Don't have the time or resources to integrate	✔	✔
5	We don't know how to work together:		
	• limited knowledge of each other's programmes	✔	✔
	• lack of skills in development work		✔
	• limited skills in partnership working		✔
6	We don't see it as a priority	✔	✔
7	We don't know with whom to work		✔
8	They're different from us	✔	✔
9	They don't understand us	✔	✔
10	They don't like us		✔
11	We don't like them	✔	
12	We don't have any autonomy at a local level		✔
13	There is limited incentive to work jointly	✔	✔

5

Achieving more effective joint working

The task ahead

The earlier chapters of the report demonstrate clearly:

- the value to be gained for area regeneration *and* for wider social inclusion initiatives from working more closely together; and
- the wide range of difficulties that confront area-based and other social inclusion initiatives becoming more integrated for the benefit of their respective clients.

The purpose of this final chapter is to explore some of the things that need to happen if the barriers are to be removed or reduced, and a greater degree of joint working encouraged. We do this by considering the steps that need to be taken at *local* and *national* levels.

Action needed at a local level

Find out what is already happening locally

The first step to improving the local coordination and integration of social inclusion programmes is ensuring that there is a clear understanding of what is happening locally. If neighbourhood regeneration initiatives are to work more effectively with wider social inclusion efforts, such as welfare-to-work programmes, there needs to be a structured dissemination of information about their aims, objectives and spheres of operation. This is vital because joint working can only be justified when it adds value, and the scope for adding value needs to be visible. Local Strategic Partnerships (LSPs) in England and Community Planning Partnerships

(CPPs) in Scotland are charged with drawing together information on relevant service delivery at the local level. However, these tend to be snapshots and a more dynamic process of knowledge exchange between the different social inclusion delivery organisations is required.

- Organisations in receipt of public money – local, national or European – should have an obligation to inform other local social inclusion players about what they offer and to whom.
- Changes in any of the operational arrangements should be communicated to key partners at the same time as they are disseminated within a particular organisation.
- Organisations should clearly designate a single point of contact for other social inclusion organisations and individuals that may wish to contact them.

There is currently no clear mechanism in place to facilitate these processes, although the development of more effective IT systems, such as the one coming on stream for Jobcentre Plus, may help. The establishment of a knowledge management system, ideally web-based, would enable easy and effective sharing of information across partners. At the same time, it would be invaluable for counsellors working on behalf of individual clients and trying to source support services relevant to the individual's needs.

Take practical steps to develop joint working between local organisations

A range of measures can be introduced to encourage joint working between neighbourhood-based, welfare-to-work and other social inclusion interventions. These practical steps are particularly important because, as described earlier, there are major cultural and organisational barriers between the different agencies and staff delivering area-based and wider social inclusion programmes.

Promote overlapping board membership

Board membership generates knowledge and ownership. For example, it should become common practice for Jobcentre Plus district managers and Jobcentre managers to be on the boards of neighbourhood regeneration initiatives, and vice versa in relation to New Deal Strategic Partnerships, Employment Zones, and so on.

Hold joint strategy meetings

Joint strategy meetings bring together key players, provide a local overview and develop understanding between organisations of their respective roles. It is important to involve key decision makers in meetings. Interaction at a strategic level sets the conditions which make it easier for operational staff in different programmes and agencies to work together, and may even require them to do this.

Promote greater operational integration

A range of mechanisms can be used to encourage joint working between operational staff:

- Secondments develop understanding across organisations and create effective bridges between them.
- It is helpful to have initiatives physically located within the same premises. This facilitates sharing of information and experience, and establishes the idea of working together for clients.
- Simple and traditional measures can help develop and cement relationships between neighbourhood regeneration and welfare-to-work staff. These would include mechanisms such as joint workshops and training sessions.
- Building the partnership-working skills of operational staff is also needed, and could again be done jointly across neighbourhood regeneration, welfare-to-work and other social

inclusion initiatives. The ambitions set out in *The learning curve* (ODPM, 2002) target many of the relevant issues for staff engaged in neighbourhood renewal, but this needs to be broadened to include those involved in other inclusion initiatives, such as staff delivering the raft of DWP-funded employment programmes.

Capture and share the tangible benefits of integrated working

For operational staff, it is important to collate and disseminate examples of how joint working with other organisations can benefit:

- their clients; and
- themselves through more effective performance and reduced costs in terms of their time.

Documentation of the practical benefits of joint working is of particular importance when there is limited awareness of other organisations, and even suspicion of the motivation and scepticism about the value of other players – a situation that tends to characterise the interface between neighbourhood regeneration and welfare-to-work interventions.

Promote joint working through intermediary organisations

A number of examples have been given of the value of intermediary organisations in helping to join up the services of neighbourhood regeneration and welfare-to-work initiatives at a local level. It is a difficult and skilled job to bring these services together effectively, but it is a job that can be carried out by well-positioned and intelligently staffed intermediaries.

Create a more comprehensive and 'Best Value' social inclusion delivery service

Start with the needs of the customers

From a neighbourhood regeneration perspective, a key exercise is to assess the extent to which local residents of working age are able to access welfare-to-work programmes which can help progress them into sustainable employment, or other inclusion services that will assist their clients. This raises questions about both eligibility criteria for programmes and the effectiveness of the services available. The same issues apply when viewed from the perspective of the customers of the national social inclusion programmes such as the New Deals. Many need help with basic skills, managing addictions, and so on, but in most areas there is rarely a comprehensive mapping of services.

Ensure all the required services are available

Where the services are clearly mapped out, neighbourhood regeneration initiatives need to get together with their counterparts running the New Deal, the Employment Zones and similar programmes to identify service gaps. The solution to plugging the gaps may not be down to local decisions, but the knowledge and expertise to identify the gaps lie within localities.

Rationalise service delivery to maximise value for money

As well as identifying gaps, unproductive service overlaps also need to be identified and tackled. There was a strong feeling across the case study localities included in this study that there needed to be a rationalisation of programmes and organisations. Currently, for example, too many organisations are perceived to be delivering the same type of employment-related programmes. This mitigates against joint working as organisations in competition do not readily work together, and it adds to the confusion for frontline staff trying to identify appropriate services for their clients.

Build more effective referral processes to maximise access to services

Once a more effective pattern of inclusion services is established, there is still a need to build more effective referral processes. However, the processes of ensuring that all the main services are in place and reducing the most extreme forms of wasteful competition remove a number of the main barriers to effective referral between agencies. Additionally, funders need to ensure that the way they fund encourages organisations to pass clients on to agencies more

able to meet their needs, rather than hold on to them.

Drive the process by aligning the key funders

The efforts of LSPs and CPPs can help set a framework for the achievement of these objectives, but in reality it will need a *concerted* and *ongoing process* led by the *funders* of key services to convert local strategic *frameworks* into more effective local *delivery* to promote neighbourhood regeneration and social inclusion more generally.

Action needed at a national level

Become more joined up at the centre, and require this down the line

Government departments need to work together more effectively before local integration can become the norm. Regional arms of central government and regional assemblies/parliaments could help play the joining-up role, but there is little evidence that this has been achieved to any great degree to date in the interface between neighbourhood regeneration and wider social inclusion initiatives. It remains to be seen whether the RCU, the Neighbourhood Renewal Unit and the Neighbourhood Renewal Teams can drive this coordination and integration agenda in a more effective manner.

Indeed, it could be argued that the lack of transparently committed integration of effort between central government departments sends negative messages down to regional and local tiers. Precisely because neighbourhood regeneration and wider social inclusion initiatives are designed, resourced and directed by different ministries, a more *transparently* joined-up approach to joint working at the national level is essential. The different departments and, where relevant, their delivery agencies (such as Jobcentre Plus) need to:

- underline jointly the importance of integrating more effectively these different types of social inclusion programme;
- communicate the importance of this to all their staff working in these areas;

- put in place systems to review the effectiveness of joint working.

Working together more effectively and openly at the national level would in turn influence and give greater credibility to a more joined-up approach at a local level.

A more practical manifestation of this would be to introduce a process of convergence in terms of funding systems and their associated administrative demands. One of the most consistently cited barriers to integration at the local level is the pain involved in responding to different sets of demands on performance indicators, financial reporting procedures, auditing requirements, and so on. These systems are set nationally and need to be redesigned to increase local benefit rather than conform to national departmental organisational norms.

Give the flexibility to local delivery to promote effective joint working

Local offices of national agencies need to have the flexibility to localise aspects of their delivery if they are to be meaningful partners in a joint attack on social exclusion and neighbourhood decline. In the body of the report, there were a number of examples of the problems faced by neighbourhood regeneration initiatives coming up against inflexible operating rules and eligibility criteria set at the national level – and a number of the funding streams intended to resource neighbourhood regeneration interventions have their own inflexibilities.

One of the emerging positive developments is the growing local flexibility within Jobcentre Plus, as many of the criticisms raised about rigidity of behaviour related to the two organisations – Employment Service and Benefits Agency – which came together to form Jobcentre Plus. The 2003 Budget signalled the introduction of increased local discretion from April 2004, including more say for:

- Jobcentre Plus district managers over the allocation of resources to tackle specific local barriers to employment;
- personal advisors over which clients can gain early entry to New Deal.

Also from April 2004, a more intensive service will be offered to jobless people in 12 of the most deprived neighbourhoods across the country to help them access employment. Within this, a discretionary fund will be available for use in each neighbourhood to give personal advisors the scope, working alongside the various players involved in LSPs, to customise solutions to employment barriers faced by their clients.

These developments describe two types of local flexibility:

- greater scope for area or district managers of national agencies to allocate the resources available to deliver mainstream services in ways which could provide more effective support for neighbourhood regeneration;
- empowerment of client-facing staff to develop and deliver customised services that cater more effectively for their clients' needs.

In these circumstances, both managerial and frontline staff of national agencies are then able to play a more active partnership role with their counterparts in other organisations in promoting a more concerted approach to neighbourhood regeneration.

Set joint targets, and make organisations jointly responsible for meeting them

The development of integrated working is inhibited by a failure to set targets that can be shared, so that there are measurable gains for all partners involved. It needs to be in the interests of the various social inclusion players to engage with other agencies to deliver more effective services for their clients. Exhortation is not sufficient. For example, if Jobcentre Plus and area regeneration initiatives had a joint responsibility for delivering the employment targets for an area or client group, this would facilitate joint working. This would require – and drive – a considerable shift in both organisational culture and processes.

The service level agreement between Jobcentre Plus and the local economic development companies (LEDCs) in Glasgow – which allows both to share job outcomes – should be applied to all area regeneration initiatives as a useful mechanism for promoting the joining up of the two approaches. The unemployed resident of a regeneration area gets a job, and all supporting players receive an organisational benefit through a contribution to their targets. This reduces the drive towards the competition for clients and employer vacancies, and avoids unnecessary duplication of services. This specific example can be applied to joining up the services of area-based initiatives and a range of other interventions in the fields of education, health, and so on. National agencies and government departments have it within their power to promote these types of arrangements. At the same time, however, the implications for the levels of targets set and the resources required to reach collective targets would need to be thought through.

There is also scope to work through the new points-based system for prioritising different clients introduced by Jobcentre Plus. There is an obvious addition that can be made to this by introducing extra points when the residents of regeneration areas are placed in work. By the same token, these area regeneration initiatives could look to see whether they can give priority to some of the specific groups prioritised by the Jobcentre Plus points system.

Clearly joint target setting is a more complex process than establishing marks that individual organisations are required to meet. It could be argued that it simply leads to double counting, but this happens already in many areas of social inclusion activity; with joint targets there would be an explicit recognition of this. These are difficult but manageable issues.

Drive joint working down through national organisations

There is a need for individual departments and agencies to provide clearer guidelines for joint working across agencies. This is an area characterised by a lot of rhetoric but limited operational guidance. Each central government department or agency with either area regeneration or wider social inclusion responsibilities should come together and agree what is expected of local projects, district offices, and so on in terms of joint working, and design a checklist stipulating a number of good practice processes. This not only provides guidance to local bodies on how to work together more effectively, but also sets a standard against which

local delivery bodies could be audited to test their effort and effectiveness in more integrated working.

A key additional step is to implement human resource management systems that drive the process of joint working down to the staff managing and delivering at the local level. If joint working is to grow in importance within the agencies and departments responsible for designing and delivering area regeneration, welfare-to-work and other social inclusion initiatives and programmes, this must be reflected in the key human resource management processes, including:

- training and development
- performance appraisal
- promotion and reward.

It is through these sorts of mechanisms that more integrated working becomes embedded in the operational staff of the main organisations. Exhortations and appeals for 'joined-up working' by politicians and senior managers are not enough – in fact not nearly enough. Although *The learning curve* has begun the process of taking forward the training and development issues, more work has to be done on the other parts of the human resource development and management process.

Create more stability in the initiative landscape

This is a very simple recommendation. Many of the factors which impede more effective joint working are either directly or indirectly a manifestation of:

- a proliferation of initiatives targeting overlapping client groups;
- the creation of too many new initiatives, confusing an already complex scene;
- an ongoing process of changing rules and regulations within specific programmes;
- insufficient attention paid to what already exists in the design of new initiatives.

From this situation flows a number of the difficulties that individuals working within area-based initiatives confront in trying to integrate more effectively with welfare-to-work and other social inclusion programmes, including:

- not knowing enough about or failing to understand fully the range of programmes operating in their areas;
- confronting programmes with priorities, time-scales and specific targets which do not align.

Given that there are already other gulfs of understanding and culture between, particularly, neighbourhood regeneration and welfare-to-work initiatives, the constant process of change works against the development of more integrated approaches at the local level.

There are a number of things that have to happen here, including:

- a reduction in the development of new initiatives;
- an analysis of the scope for rationalising existing initiatives;
- a more careful approach to changing the rules of specific programmes.

Make integration a key programme design and redesign component

It is unrealistic, of course, to expect a significant slow-down in the development of new social inclusion initiatives. In the absence of this, the government needs to require its policy and programme developers to build in integration as a key design feature. In other words, alongside any other design specifications, new programmes should be required to demonstrate:

- a clear awareness of competing and complementary provision in terms of client, and type of service; and
- how the programme has been designed to realise the potential for integration with other social inclusion interventions.

In a sense, programme appraisal mechanisms must include integration as a central criterion that needs to be met in the same way as strategic fit, value for money, sustainability, and so on.

We have now reached the stage where, before national government departments introduce any new initiatives which impact on specific localities, they should be required to either:

- bring to an end one or more of the existing initiatives in that locality; or
- show in a clearly articulated plan how the new initiative will interface with and add value to the initiatives that already exist.

The RCU (2002b) has already issued strong guidance for government departments considering new area-based initiatives or expansions to existing ones. The key issue is the rigour with which this process is managed and monitored, particularly in terms of the interface with mainstream delivery through agencies such as Jobcentre Plus, health trusts, and so on.

Overview

The research uncovered many positive examples of organisations trying – and often successfully – to work together more effectively to benefit their clients from the more socially excluded neighbourhoods and groups of the population. The reality is that many of the good practice features embedded in national initiatives for neighbourhood regeneration and social inclusion more generally were first developed by local organisations trying to solve local problems. The same spirit and preparedness to work against the odds is still out there.

National government and its agencies must take more responsibility for creating a framework for local action and a set of programmes and funding streams which are in broad alignment in terms of their operating rules, administrative arrangements and other features which can act as barriers to joint working. To date, the focus of government effort in the area of joint working has been to create coordination machinery – effectively organisations which neither make policy and design programmes, nor fund service delivery. Additionally, these coordinating bodies tend to sit within specific government departments, and inevitably their leverage on other departments is diminished.

What is required at this time is for the main national government departments involved directly or indirectly in promoting neighbourhood regeneration and social inclusion more generally to come together in order to:

- rationalise the plethora of initiatives and programmes;
- remove the design features of programmes which raise the greatest barriers to joint working at the local level;
- introduce joint target setting, where possible, into cognate departments and agencies, with the opportunity to share positive outcomes the flip-side of the coin;
- produce clear guidance to all staff in their respective organisations that joint working is a central ethos;
- redesign staff training, appraisal and other human resource management processes to underline the importance of joint working to every employee.

None of this is rocket science, but it requires the acceptance at a high level of government that a more effective prosecution of the war against social exclusion requires:

- *less* by way of exhortation to work together, backed up by a growing set of coordination arrangements;
- *more* by way of a serious attempt to make hard decisions at the centre on reducing the volume of social inclusion programmes and minimising their administrative diversity to make it easier for people at the local level to get on and do the job.

References

Audit Commission (2002) *Policy focus neighbourhood renewal*, London: Audit Commission.

Carley, M., Chapman, M., Hastings, A., Kirk, K. and Young, R. (2000) *Urban regeneration through partnership: A study in nine urban regions in England, Scotland and Wales*, Bristol/York: The Policy Press/Joseph Rowntree Foundation.

DETR (Department for the Environment, Transport and the Regions) (2000) *Joining it up locally,* Report of Policy Action Team 17, London: DETR.

DfES (Department for Education and Science) (2002) *Report on the Review of Learning Partnerships*, London: DfES.

DTLR (Department for Transport, Local Government and the Regions), Local Government Association and the Treasury (2001) *Local Public Service Agreements: New challenges*, London: DTLR.

DTLR (2002) *Collaboration and coordination in area based initiatives*, London: Neighbourhood Renewal Unit and RCU.

DWP (Department for Work and Pensions) (2001) *Towards full employment in a modern society*, London: DWP.

Lloyd, M., Illsley, B. and Graham, F. (2001) *Community planning in Scotland: A final report to the Community Planning Task Force Project*, Dundee: University of Dundee.

Maclennan, D. (2000) *Changing places, engaging people*, York: Joseph Rowntree Foundation.

ODPM (Office of the Deputy Prime Minister) (2002) *The learning curve: Developing skills and knowledge for neighbourhood renewal*, London: Neighbourhood Renewal Unit.

Performance and Innovation Unit (2000) *Reaching out: The role of central government at a regional and local level*, London: Cabinet Office.

RCU (Regional Co-ordination Unit) (2002a) *Review of area based initiatives*, London: RCU.

RCU (2002b) *Guidance on the coordination of area based initiatives*, London: RCU.

Rodger, J., Burniston, S. and Lawless, M. (2000) *The interaction of national and local employment policies: Practice and outcomes*, DfEE RR214, London: DfEE.

Scottish Executive (2002) *Better communities in Scotland: Closing the gap*, Edinburgh: Scottish Executive.

SEU (Social Exclusion Unit) (2000) *National Strategy for Neighbourhood Renewal for England and Wales*, London: SEU.

SEU (2001) *A new commitment to neighbourhood renewal: National Strategy action plan*, London: SEU.

Smith, G. (1999) 'Area based initiatives: the rationale and options for area targeting', CASE Paper 25, London: Centre for Analysis of Social Exclusion, London School of Economics and Political Science.

Tavistock Institute (1999) *New Deal for Young Unemployed People: National case studies of delivery and impact*, ESR 30, London: Employment Service.